WOULD YOU RATHER BABY EIDITION

A FUNNY GAME FOR NEW PARENTS

KIT PENN

WOULD YOU RATHER? BABY EDITION

1. Would You Rather? 1
2. RIdiculous Scenarios 2
   Time to Get Serious! 12
   What Would you do? The baby years! 28
   What Would you do? Toddler and beyond! 37
3. The Important Questions 41
   Things we should discuss 43

CHAPTER ONE
WOULD YOU RATHER?

Get ready to dive into the hilarious, sometimes absurd, and occasionally all-too-real world of parenting dilemmas!

In this chapter, we'll test your decision-making skills with Would You Rather? *and* What Would You do? *scenarios that range from laugh-out-loud ridiculous to "this could actually happen" moments.*

But life as a new parent isn't just about the giggles. Sometimes, it's important to pause and reflect. That's where our Time to Get Serious! *questions come in. These deeper prompts will help you and your loved ones consider how to handle the challenges and joys of raising a child from the baby bubble through to the challenging teenage years.*

So grab a hot drink, your partner or loved ones, and prepare to laugh, cringe, and maybe even learn something along the way.

Let's play!

CHAPTER TWO
RIDICULOUS SCENARIOS

WOULD YOU RATHER...

...HAVE AN OUTDOOR PLAYDATE OR AN INDOOR PLAYDATE?

WOULD YOU RATHER...

...CLEAN UP BABY SICK ON YOUR FAVOURITE SHIRT OR FISH A PACIFIER OUT OF A PUBLIC TOILET?

WOULD YOU RATHER...

...CHANGE A DIAPER AFTER A BABY HAS EATEN A WHOLE JAR OF PRUNES OR BATHE A BABY COVERED HEAD-TO-TOE IN SPAGHETTI SAUCE?

WOULD YOU RATHER...

...DEAL WITH A BABY WHO HAS LEARNED HOW TO OPEN EVERY CUPBOARD OR ONE WHO CLIMBS ON EVERYTHING LIKE A LITTLE NINJA?

WOULD YOU RATHER...

...HAVE A BABY WHO CRIES WHENEVER SOMEONE ELSE HOLDS THEM OR ONE WHO IMMEDIATELY WANTS TO BE HELD BY EVERYONE EXCEPT YOU?

WOULD YOU RATHER...

...HAVE TO GET UP EARLY AND GET THE BABY DRESSED AND SORT THEIR BREAKFAST EVERY MORNING, OR BE THE ONE THAT HAS TO DO THEIR DINNER, BATH, BOOKS AND BEDTIME EVERY NIGHT?

WOULD YOU RATHER...

...HAVE A BABY WHO FINDS IT HILARIOUS TO THROW THINGS AT PEOPLE OR ONE WHO LIKES TO STICK THEIR TONGUE OUT AND BLOW RASPBERRIES AT EVERY PERSON THEY PASS?

WOULD YOU RATHER...

...HAVE SURPRISE TWINS OR A BABY THAT DOESN'T SLEEP FOR MORE THAN AN HOUR AT A TIME?

WOULD YOU RATHER...

...HAVE A WRIGGLY BABY WHO ONLY SLEEPS SOUNDLY IN YOUR BED OR ONE WHO INSISTS ON WAKING UP AT 5 A.M. EVERY DAY, NO MATTER WHAT?

WOULD YOU RATHER...

...SING “BABY SHARK” ON REPEAT FOR AN ENTIRE ROAD TRIP OR LISTEN TO THE SOUND OF A BEEPING TOY THAT’S STUCK ON REPEAT?

WOULD YOU RATHER...

...BE PEED ON EVERY TIME YOU CHANGE A DIAPER OR HAVE TO CLEAN UP A FOOD-SPLATTER MESS AFTER EVERY MEAL?

WOULD YOU RATHER...

...STEP ON A PIECE OF LEGO BAREFOOT IN THE DARK OR ACCIDENTALLY SPILL AN ENTIRE BOTTLE OF FORMULA ON THE CARPET?

WOULD YOU RATHER...

...HAVE YOUR BABY'S FIRST WORD BE A SWEAR WORD THEY OVERHEARD YOU SAY OR THE NAME OF SOMEONE YOU REALLY DISLIKE?

WOULD YOU RATHER...

...CLEAN UP A BLOWOUT DIAPER DURING A LONG CAR TRIP OR WHILE IN THE MIDDLE OF GROCERY SHOPPING?

WOULD YOU RATHER...

...HAVE A BABY WHO HATES BATH TIME OR WHO HATES HAVING THEIR NAPPY CHANGED?

WOULD YOU RATHER...

...BABY PEES ON YOU EVERY TIME YOU CHANGE HIM/HER OR THE BABY THROWS UP ON YOUR SHOULDER EVERY TIME YOU BURP THEM?

WOULD YOU RATHER...

...ACCIDENTALLY WEAR MISMATCHED SHOES TO WORK OR HAVE SICK ON THE BACK OF YOUR SHIRT ALL DAY WITHOUT NOTICING?

WOULD YOU RATHER...

...BE WOKEN UP AT 3 A.M. EVERY NIGHT BY YOUR BABY'S CRIES OR BY YOUR PARTNER'S SNORING?

WOULD YOU RATHER...

...HAVE TO ENTERTAIN YOUR BABY BY SINGING THE SAME SONG ON REPEAT OR HAVING TO READ THE SAME BOOK OVER AND OVER?

WOULD YOU RATHER...

...FIND YOUR BABY COVERED IN FLOUR AFTER GETTING INTO THE KITCHEN OR DISCOVER THEY'VE PULLED OUT EVERY SINGLE BABY WIPE FROM THE PACKET WHILE YOUR BACK WAS TURNED?

WOULD YOU RATHER...

...HAVE A BABY WHO ONLY NAPS IN THE CAR OR ONE WHO ONLY NAPS IN THE STROLLER?

WOULD YOU RATHER...

...HAVE A BABY WHO LOVES TO DROP EVERYTHING FROM THEIR HIGH CHAIR OR ONE WHO THROWS A TANTRUM EVERY TIME THEY'RE PUT IN IT?

WOULD YOU RATHER...

...HAVE A BABY WHO WANTS TO TASTE-TEST EVERYTHING, INCLUDING NON-FOOD ITEMS, OR ONE WHO REFUSES TO EAT ANYTHING NEW?

WOULD YOU RATHER...

...HAVE A BABY WHO IS OUTGOING, NOISY AND STUBBORN OR ONE WHO IS QUIET, SHY AND AGREEABLE?

WOULD YOU RATHER...

...HAVE A BABY WHO CRIES WHENEVER YOU SIT DOWN OR ONE WHO CRIES WHENEVER YOU STAND UP?

WOULD YOU RATHER...

...HAVE TO SING A LULLABY TO YOUR BABY IN A CROWDED SUPERMARKET OR DANCE FOR THEM IN THE MIDDLE OF A PARK?

WOULD YOU RATHER...

...HAVE A BABY WHO DEMANDS TO BE CARRIED EVERYWHERE OR ONE WHO INSISTS ON CRAWLING EVEN IN PLACES THEY SHOULDN'T?

WOULD YOU RATHER...

...HAVE TO CHASE YOUR BABY AROUND THE HOUSE TO GET THEM DRESSED OR HAVE THEM UNDRESS THEMSELVES EVERY TIME YOU TURN AROUND?

WOULD YOU RATHER...

...HAVE A BABY WHO INSISTS ON PLAYING WITH THE VACUUM CLEANER OR ONE WHO CRIES EVERY TIME YOU TURN IT ON?

WOULD YOU RATHER...

...HAVE A BABY WHO LOVES TO IMITATE ANIMAL SOUNDS ALL DAY OR ONE WHO INSISTS ON HAVING A CONVERSATION WITH YOU IN BABY BABBLE?

WOULD YOU RATHER...

...HAVE A BABY WHO ALWAYS WANTS TO HELP WITH CLEANING UP BUT MAKES AN EVEN BIGGER MESS OR ONE WHO REFUSES TO HELP BUT KEEPS THE MESS CONTAINED?

TIME TO GET SERIOUS!

WOULD YOU RATHER...

...HAVE A CHILD WHO IS NATURALLY INDEPENDENT BUT DISTANT OR ONE WHO IS VERY ATTACHED BUT MORE DEPENDENT ON YOU?

WOULD YOU RATHER...

...BE THE PARENT WHO ENFORCES RULES AND STRUCTURE OR THE ONE WHO ENCOURAGES FLEXIBILITY AND FREE PLAY?

WOULD YOU RATHER...

...RETURN TO WORK AND RELY ON DAYCARE OR STAY AT HOME FULL-TIME WITH YOUR CHILD?

WOULD YOU RATHER...

...PRIORITIZE TEACHING YOUR CHILD MANNERS FROM AN EARLY AGE OR FOCUS ON ENCOURAGING THEIR CREATIVITY AND SELF-EXPRESSION?

WOULD YOU RATHER...

...SPEND THE FIRST FEW MONTHS ADJUSTING TO LIFE AS NEW PARENTS ALONE OR HAVE FAMILY STAYING WITH YOU TO HELP (BUT ALSO IN YOUR SPACE)?

WOULD YOU RATHER...

...TEACH YOUR CHILD TO SELF-SOOTHE AT NIGHT OR ALWAYS COMFORT THEM IMMEDIATELY WHEN THEY CRY?

WOULD YOU RATHER...

...NEVER RECEIVE UNSOLICITED PARENTING ADVICE BUT FEEL UNSUPPORTED, OR GET ENDLESS ADVICE BUT FEEL LIKE PEOPLE HAVE YOUR BACK?

WOULD YOU RATHER...

...GO INTO LABOR TWO WEEKS EARLY WHEN YOU FEEL UNPREPARED OR TWO WEEKS LATE WHEN YOU'RE COMPLETELY OVER BEING PREGNANT?

WOULD YOU RATHER...

...SPEND MORE TIME FOCUSING ON YOUR CHILD'S ACADEMIC DEVELOPMENT OR THEIR EMOTIONAL AND SOCIAL SKILLS?

WOULD YOU RATHER...

...HAVE YOUR CHILD BE NATURALLY CONFIDENT BUT SOMETIMES OVERBEARING OR MORE RESERVED BUT CONSIDERATE?

WOULD YOU RATHER...

...MANAGE LIFE WITH SIGNIFICANTLY LESS PERSONAL TIME OR WITH REDUCED FINANCIAL FLEXIBILITY DUE TO ADDED CHILDCARE COSTS?

WOULD YOU RATHER...

...HAVE YOUR PARTNER MISS THE BIRTH DUE TO UNFORESEEN CIRCUMSTANCES OR MISS THE FIRST WEEK OF YOUR BABY'S LIFE BECAUSE OF WORK OR TRAVEL?

WOULD YOU RATHER...

...SPEND YOUR ENTIRE MATERNITY LEAVE IN YOUR DREAM DESTINATION BUT HAVE NO HELP, OR STAY HOME WITH LOTS OF FAMILY SUPPORT?

WOULD YOU RATHER...

...DEAL WITH A BABY WHO REFUSES TO TAKE A BOTTLE OR ONE WHO REFUSES TO BREASTFEED?

WOULD YOU RATHER...

...FOCUS ON MAINTAINING YOUR CAREER TRAJECTORY WHILE BALANCING PARENTHOOD OR PRIORITIZE BEING HOME FOR YOUR CHILD'S FIRST YEAR?

WOULD YOU RATHER...

...RAISE YOUR BABY IN A BUSY CITY WITH LOTS OF OPPORTUNITIES OR IN A QUIET RURAL AREA WITH MORE SPACE AND NATURE?

WOULD YOU RATHER...

...FOCUS ON EXPOSING YOUR CHILD TO A VARIETY OF ACTIVITIES OR CONCENTRATE ON A FEW TO HELP THEM MASTER SPECIFIC SKILLS?

WOULD YOU RATHER...

...GO ON A DATE WITH YOUR PARTNER OR FOR SOME MUCH-NEEDED ALONE TIME IF YOU WERE TO HAVE A NIGHT OFF FROM BABY DUTIES?

WOULD YOU RATHER...

...STEP IN TO PREVENT YOUR CHILD FROM HAVING A SMALL FALL OR LET THEM FALL TO TEACH THEM RESILIENCE?

WOULD YOU RATHER...

...MOVE CLOSER TO FAMILY FOR EXTRA SUPPORT BUT LEAVE YOUR COMMUNITY OR STAY WHERE YOU ARE AND MANAGE ON YOUR OWN?

WOULD YOU RATHER...

...TAKE ON MORE HOUSEHOLD RESPONSIBILITIES TO SUPPORT YOUR PARTNER OR FOCUS MORE ON SHARED PARENTING TASKS?

WOULD YOU RATHER...

...EMPHASIZE THE IMPORTANCE OF SHARING WITH YOUR CHILD OR TEACH THEM TO SET BOUNDARIES AND PROTECT THEIR OWN BELONGINGS?

WOULD YOU RATHER...

...PRIORITIZE YOUR CHILD'S PHYSICAL HEALTH AND FITNESS OR THEIR MENTAL AND EMOTIONAL WELL-BEING?

WOULD YOU RATHER...

...ENCOURAGE YOUR CHILD TO TAKE RISKS AND TRY NEW THINGS OR GUIDE THEM TO BE CAUTIOUS AND THINK BEFORE THEY ACT?

WOULD YOU RATHER...

...HAVE A CHILD WHO EXCELS IN SCHOOL BUT STRUGGLES WITH FRIENDSHIPS OR ONE WHO IS SOCIALLY POPULAR BUT STRUGGLES ACADEMICALLY?

WOULD YOU RATHER...

...ADJUST TO A REDUCED SOCIAL LIFE TO PRIORITIZE PARENTING OR MAINTAIN YOUR FRIENDSHIPS AND RELY MORE ON CHILDCARE?

WOULD YOU RATHER...

...RESTRUCTURE YOUR BUDGET TO SAVE FOR THE BABY'S FUTURE OR SPEND MORE NOW ON MAKING THE FIRST YEAR AS SMOOTH AS POSSIBLE?

WOULD YOU RATHER...

...DELAY BIG PERSONAL GOALS LIKE BUYING A HOUSE OR FOCUS ON THEM WHILE NAVIGATING THE CHALLENGES OF PARENTING?

WOULD YOU RATHER...

...EXPOSE YOUR CHILD TO DIVERSE CULTURES AND EXPERIENCES EARLY ON OR WAIT UNTIL THEY ARE OLDER TO TRAVEL AND LEARN ABOUT THE WORLD?

WOULD YOU RATHER...

...BE THE PARENT WHO IS VERY INVOLVED IN YOUR CHILD'S SCHOOL ACTIVITIES OR ONE WHO ENCOURAGES THEM TO BE INDEPENDENT IN THEIR EDUCATION?

WOULD YOU RATHER...

...FOCUS ON TEACHING YOUR CHILD TRADITIONAL VALUES OR ENCOURAGE THEM TO QUESTION NORMS AND THINK CRITICALLY?

WOULD YOU RATHER...

...HAVE YOUR CHILD EXCEL IN A SPORT OR BE PROFICIENT IN A MUSICAL INSTRUMENT?

WOULD YOU RATHER...

...PRIORITIZE TEACHING YOUR CHILD THE IMPORTANCE OF FAMILY AND COMMUNITY OR THE VALUE OF INDIVIDUALITY AND PERSONAL ACHIEVEMENT?

WOULD YOU RATHER...

...STICK WITH YOUR CURRENT ROUTINE AND ADAPT IT FOR PARENTHOOD OR COMPLETELY OVERHAUL YOUR SCHEDULE TO FIT YOUR BABY'S NEEDS?

WOULD YOU RATHER...

...LIVE NEAR A HIGH-QUALITY DAYCARE OR NEAR YOUR WORKPLACE FOR EASIER COMMUTING?

WOULD YOU RATHER...

...BE THE PARENT WHO IS ALWAYS ON TOP OF THINGS AND ORGANISED OR ONE WHO IS MORE LAID-BACK AND GOES WITH THE FLOW?

WOULD YOU RATHER...

...HAVE A CHILD WHO IS CURIOUS AND ASKS LOTS OF QUESTIONS OR ONE WHO IS CONTENT AND EASY-GOING BUT LESS INQUISITIVE?

WOULD YOU RATHER...

...HAVE YOUR CHILD BE A LEADER IN THEIR PEER GROUP BUT OCCASIONALLY BOSSY OR A TEAM PLAYER WHO SOMETIMES FOLLOWS THE CROWD?

WOULD YOU RATHER...

...ADJUST A HOBBY SO YOUR BABY CAN JOIN YOU OR CONTINUE TO DO THE HOBBY JUST FOR YOURSELF BUT LESS FREQUENTLY?

WOULD YOU RATHER...

...BE THE PARENT WHO SETS STRICT SCREEN TIME LIMITS OR THE ONE WHO USES TECHNOLOGY AS A TOOL FOR LEARNING AND ENTERTAINMENT?

WOULD YOU RATHER...

...FOCUS ON PREPARING YOUR CHILD FOR THE CHALLENGES OF ADULTHOOD EARLY ON OR LET THEM ENJOY THEIR CHILDHOOD WITHOUT TOO MANY RESPONSIBILITIES?

WOULD YOU RATHER...

...RELY ON FRIENDS AND FAMILY FOR SUPPORT WHEN YOU NEED BREAKS OR HIRE PROFESSIONAL HELP TO MAINTAIN INDEPENDENCE?

WOULD YOU RATHER...

...FOCUS ON KEEPING YOUR ROMANTIC RELATIONSHIP STRONG DURING THE FIRST YEAR OR PRIORITIZE INDIVIDUAL SELF-CARE TO STAY BALANCED?

WOULD YOU RATHER...

...HAVE A CHILD WHO IS HIGHLY MOTIVATED AND AMBITIOUS BUT OFTEN STRESSED, OR ONE WHO IS RELAXED AND CONTENT BUT LESS DRIVEN?

WOULD YOU RATHER...

...TEACH YOUR CHILD THE VALUE OF SAVING MONEY EARLY ON OR ENCOURAGE THEM TO SPEND ON EXPERIENCES AND THINGS THEY ENJOY?

WOULD YOU RATHER...

...HAVE A COMPLETELY UNMEDICATED LABOR THAT LASTS 24 HOURS OR A SHORTER, HIGHLY MEDICATED BIRTH WITH MORE RECOVERY TIME?

WOULD YOU RATHER...

...HAVE FEWER DATE NIGHTS FOR THE FIRST YEAR OR LESS TIME TO PURSUE PERSONAL INTERESTS OUTSIDE OF PARENTING?

WOULD YOU RATHER...

...BE THE PARENT WHO ALWAYS SETS A GOOD EXAMPLE THROUGH YOUR ACTIONS OR ONE WHO IS MORE OPEN ABOUT YOUR MISTAKES AND LEARNING EXPERIENCES?

WOULD YOU RATHER...

...ENCOURAGE YOUR CHILD TO PURSUE A CAREER THAT IS STABLE AND SECURE OR ONE THAT ALIGNS WITH THEIR PASSIONS, EVEN IF IT'S LESS PREDICTABLE?

WOULD YOU RATHER...

...HAVE A CHILD WHO IS VERY NEAT AND ORGANIZED BUT SOMETIMES RIGID OR ONE WHO IS CREATIVE AND MESSY BUT FLEXIBLE?

WHAT WOULD YOU DO? THE BABY YEARS!

YOUR BABY SPITS UP ALL OVER YOUR LAST CLEAN SHIRT FIVE MINUTES BEFORE YOU'RE SUPPOSED TO LEAVE THE HOUSE FOR WORK.

WHAT WOULD YOU DO?

IT'S 3 A.M., AND YOUR BABY WON'T STOP CRYING NO MATTER WHAT YOU TRY.

WHAT WOULD YOU DO?

YOU'RE AT A RESTAURANT, AND YOUR BABY HAS A BLOWOUT DIAPER. THERE'S NO CHANGING TABLE IN THE RESTROOM.

YOU FINALLY GET THE BABY DOWN FOR A NAP, BUT YOUR NEIGHBOR STARTS MOWING THEIR LAWN.

WHAT WOULD YOU DO?

YOUR BABY HAS A SPECIAL OCCASION AT THEIR NURSERY, BUT IT CLASHES WITH AN IMPORTANT MEETING.

WHAT WOULD YOU DO?

YOU REALIZE HALFWAY THROUGH A CAR TRIP THAT YOU FORGOT THE DIAPER BAG.

WHAT WOULD YOU DO?

EVERYONE IN THE HOUSE GETS SICK AT THE SAME TIME.

WHAT WOULD YOU DO?

YOU'RE MEETING FRIENDS FOR COFFEE, AND YOUR BABY THROWS UP ON YOUR FRIEND'S SHIRT.

WHAT WOULD YOU DO?

YOUR BABY REFUSES TO SLEEP ANYWHERE BUT IN YOUR ARMS.

WHAT WOULD YOU DO?

YOU'RE AT THE PARK, AND ANOTHER CHILD TRIES TO TAKE A TOY AWAY FROM YOUR BABY.

WHAT WOULD YOU DO?

YOU REALLY WANT TO SEE A FRIEND, BUT THE ONLY TIME THEY OFFER TO MEET IS DURING BEDTIME WHEN YOUR BABY NEEDS YOU.

WHAT WOULD YOU DO?

YOUR BABY DEVELOPS A RASH, AND YOU'RE NOT SURE IF IT'S SERIOUS.

WHAT WOULD YOU DO?

YOU'RE HOSTING GUESTS, AND YOUR BABY HAS A MELTDOWN AND IT STOPS BEING FUN FOR YOU.

WHAT WOULD YOU DO?

YOU DROP YOUR BABY'S FAVORITE PACIFIER ON THE FLOOR, AND THERE'S NO WAY TO CLEAN IT.

WHAT WOULD YOU DO?

YOU'VE BEEN LOOKING AFTER A GRUMPY BABY ALL DAY WHEN A LOVED ONE SWINGS BY AND OFFERS TO GIVE YOU AN HOUR OFF.

WHAT WOULD YOU DO?

YOUR BABY WON'T STOP GIGGLING WHEN YOU'RE TRYING TO GET THEM TO SLEEP.

WHAT WOULD YOU DO?

YOUR BABY'S DIAPER LEAKS ONTO A FRIEND'S COUCH.

WHAT WOULD YOU DO?

YOU'RE ON A VIDEO CALL FOR WORK, AND YOUR BABY STARTS CRYING IN THE BACKGROUND.

WHAT WOULD YOU DO?

YOUR BABY DROPS THEIR FAVORITE TOY OUT OF THE STROLLER, AND YOU DON'T REALIZE IT UNTIL MUCH LATER.

WHAT WOULD YOU DO?

YOU'RE GIVING YOUR BABY A BATH, AND THEY SUDDENLY DECIDE IT'S THE PERFECT TIME TO POOP.

WHAT WOULD YOU DO?

YOU ARE PARENTING WITH A PARTNER, AND YOU BOTH FEEL TIRED, HAVE BARELY ANY TIME TO SEE EACH OTHER AND START ARGUING.

WHAT WOULD YOU DO?

ONE OF YOUR CLOSET FRIENDS HAS A BABY AT THE SAME TIME, BUT WHEN YOU MEET, YOU FEEL THAT ALL THEY TALK ABOUT IS THEIR OWN BABY.

WHAT WOULD YOU DO?

YOU'RE HAVING A RARE DATE NIGHT, BUT THE BABYSITTER TEXTS THAT THE BABY WON'T STOP CRYING.

WHAT WOULD YOU DO?

YOU'RE VISITING FAMILY, AND THEY KEEP GIVING YOU UNSOLICITED PARENTING ADVICE.

WHAT WOULD YOU DO?

YOUR BABY FALLS ASLEEP IN THEIR HIGH CHAIR HALFWAY THROUGH EATING.

WHAT WOULD YOU DO?

SINCE BECOMING PARENTS, YOU FEEL LIKE SOME OF YOUR FRIENDS DON'T MAKE ANY EFFORT TO SEE YOU ANY MORE.

WHAT WOULD YOU DO?

YOU ARE PARENTING WITH A PARTNER AND BOTH PARENTS GET INVITED TO A PARTY THAT THEY BOTH REALLY WANT TO GO TO, BUT NO SITTERS ARE AVAILABLE.

WHAT WOULD YOU DO?

YOU'VE SPENT TIME MAKING A NUTRITIOUS HOMEMADE PURÉE FOR YOUR BABY, BUT THEY REFUSE TO TAKE EVEN ONE SPOONFUL AND START FLINGING IT OFF THEIR HIGH CHAIR.

WHAT WOULD YOU DO?

YOUR BABY WAKES UP FOR THE DAY AN HOUR EARLIER THAN USUAL, AND YOU'VE BARELY SLEPT. YOU'RE UTTERLY EXHAUSTED, BUT THEY'RE WIDE AWAKE AND FULL OF ENERGY.

WHAT WOULD YOU DO?

EVERY TIME YOU STRAP YOUR BABY INTO THEIR CAR SEAT, THEY CRY AS IF THE WORLD IS ENDING, EVEN FOR A QUICK TRIP.

WHAT WOULD YOU DO?

A STRANGER APPROACHES IN A CAFÉ AND TRIES TO PAT YOUR BABY'S HEAD OR PINCH THEIR CHEEK, MAKING YOU UNCOMFORTABLE.

WHAT WOULD YOU DO?

WHAT WOULD YOU DO? TODDLER AND BEYOND!

A FAMILY MEMBER REALLY WANTS TO BUY THEM A PRESENT THAT YOU FEEL IS INAPPROPRIATE.

WHAT WOULD YOU DO?

YOUR CHILD INSISTS ON HAVING A PET ROCK OR AN IMAGINARY FRIEND.

WHAT WOULD YOU DO?

YOUR CHILD WANTS TO DECORATE THEIR PERSONAL SPACE WITH POSTERS AND ITEMS YOU FIND TOO BOLD OR COLORFUL.

WHAT WOULD YOU DO?

YOUR CHILD IS DESPERATE TO HAVE A PET RABBIT.

WHAT WOULD YOU DO?

YOUR CHILD IS STRUGGLING WITH BULLYING AT SCHOOL, AND YOU'RE NOT SURE HOW TO BEST SUPPORT THEM.

WHAT WOULD YOU DO?

YOUR TEENAGER STARTS SHOWING INTEREST IN ACTIVITIES OR FRIENDS YOU DISAPPROVE OF.

WHAT WOULD YOU DO?

YOUR CHILD REFUSES TO DO THEIR HOMEWORK, IMPACTING THEIR GRADES.

WHAT WOULD YOU DO?

YOUR CHILD WANTS TO STAY OUT LATE WITH FRIENDS, BUT YOU'RE CONCERNED ABOUT THEIR SAFETY.

WHAT WOULD YOU DO?

YOUR CHILD EXPRESSES INTEREST IN A CAREER PATH THAT'S UNCONVENTIONAL OR RISKY.

WHAT WOULD YOU DO?

YOU ARE PARENTING WITH A PARTNER, AND BOTH OF YOU START TO FEEL LIKE THE OTHER ISN'T PULLING THEIR WEIGHT AS A PARENT.

WHAT WOULD YOU DO?

YOUR CHILD STARTS USING SOCIAL MEDIA EXCESSIVELY, AND YOU'RE WORRIED ABOUT THEIR ONLINE SAFETY.

WHAT WOULD YOU DO?

YOUR CHILD IS NOT INTERESTED IN JOINING IN FAMILY ACTIVITIES ANYMORE.

WHAT WOULD YOU DO?

YOUR CHILD WANTS TO REARRANGE THEIR BEDROOM LAYOUT, MOVING FURNITURE TO UNCONVENTIONAL PLACES.

WHAT WOULD YOU DO?

YOUR CHILD WANTS TO SKIP A FAMILY DINNER TO HANG OUT WITH FRIENDS INSTEAD.

WHAT WOULD YOU DO?

CHAPTER THREE
THE IMPORTANT QUESTIONS

Becoming a parent is a profound journey—not just for the child you're bringing into the world but for you as an individual and as a partner. We've had some fun with this book so far. But now it's a time to reflect on your own upbringing, explore what shaped you into the person you are today, and decide what kind of parent you want to become.

Grab your partner, a loved one or a journal, and work through the questions.

This section is designed to help you (and your partner if you're doing this with someone else) dive deeper into meaningful conversations about childhood experiences, family values, and your vision for parenting. These questions encourage you to share stories, uncover beliefs, and align on how you'll navigate this new chapter.

Understanding your own (and each other's) background, hopes, and fears can create strong foundations as a parent. These discussions might reveal unexpected insights or challenges, but they'll also help you grow closer as a team, prepared to nurture and guide your child through life.

Take your time with these questions. Be open, honest, and curious about your answers. Together, you're not only shaping the life of your child but also creating a legacy rooted in love, understanding, and shared values.

THINGS WE SHOULD DISCUSS

WHAT IS ONE THING YOUR PARENTS DID THAT YOU WANT TO REPLICATE WHEN RAISING YOUR CHILD, AND ONE THING YOU'D LIKE TO DO DIFFERENTLY?

HOW DID YOUR PARENTS HANDLE DISCIPLINE, AND DO YOU THINK THAT APPROACH WOULD WORK FOR YOU, OR DO YOU WANT TO TRY SOMETHING DIFFERENT?

WHAT WAS YOUR FAVOURITE CHILDHOOD MEMORY, AND HOW CAN YOU CREATE SIMILAR EXPERIENCES FOR YOUR CHILD?

WHAT DO YOU THINK WILL BE YOUR BIGGEST STRENGTH AS A PARENT, AND WHERE DO YOU THINK YOU MIGHT STRUGGLE?

HOW DID YOUR PARENTS SHOW LOVE AND AFFECTION, AND HOW DO YOU WANT TO EXPRESS THAT TO YOUR CHILD?

WERE THERE ANY TRADITIONS OR ROUTINES FROM YOUR CHILDHOOD THAT YOU'D LIKE TO CONTINUE OR START WITH YOUR FAMILY?

HOW DO YOU THINK YOUR UPBRINGING INFLUENCED YOUR VIEWS ON PARENTING, AND WHAT BELIEFS DO YOU WANT TO PASS ON TO YOUR CHILD?

WHAT'S SOMETHING YOU WISH YOUR PARENTS HAD DONE MORE OF WHEN YOU WERE GROWING UP, AND HOW CAN YOU ENSURE YOUR CHILD FEELS SUPPORTED IN THAT AREA?

DO YOU REMEMBER ANY FEARS OR ANXIETIES YOU HAD AS A CHILD, AND HOW CAN YOU HELP YOUR CHILD FEEL SAFE AND SECURE?

WHAT QUALITIES DO YOU THINK ARE MOST IMPORTANT IN A PARENT, AND WHICH ONES DO YOU FEEL CONFIDENT IN, AND WHICH MIGHT BE CHALLENGING FOR YOU?

[FOR THOSE WHO HAVE SIBLINGS] WHAT ROLE DID YOUR SIBLINGS PLAY IN YOUR UPBRINGING, AND HOW DO YOU THINK THAT EXPERIENCE WILL INFLUENCE HOW YOU HANDLE SIBLING DYNAMICS WITH YOUR OWN CHILDREN?

[FOR THOSE WHO WERE ONLY CHILDREN] HOW WAS THE EXPERIENCE FOR YOU GROWING UP AS AN ONLY CHILD, AND WILL THAT IMPACT THE WAY YOU THINK ABOUT HAVING MORE THAN ONE CHILD YOURSELF?

HOW DID YOUR FAMILY HANDLE CONFLICT AND DISAGREEMENTS, AND WHAT APPROACH DO YOU THINK WILL WORK BEST FOR YOU WHEN IT COMES TO PARENTING?

WHAT DID YOU ENJOY DOING MOST WITH YOUR PARENTS AS A CHILD, AND HOW CAN YOU INCORPORATE SIMILAR ACTIVITIES INTO YOUR FAMILY LIFE?

WERE THERE ANY CHALLENGES YOUR PARENTS FACED THAT YOU THINK YOU MIGHT ALSO ENCOUNTER, AND HOW CAN YOU PREPARE FOR THEM?

HOW DID YOUR PARENTS ENCOURAGE YOUR INTERESTS AND HOBBIES, AND WHAT'S ONE WAY YOU WANT TO SUPPORT YOUR CHILD'S PASSIONS?

WHAT WERE YOUR PARENTS' BIGGEST STRENGTHS AS CAREGIVERS, AND HOW DO YOU SEE THOSE QUALITIES MANIFESTING IN YOURSELF?

DID YOU HAVE A CLOSE BOND WITH YOUR GRANDPARENTS OR OTHER EXTENDED FAMILY MEMBERS, AND HOW DO YOU ENVISION YOUR CHILD'S RELATIONSHIP WITH THEIR EXTENDED FAMILY?

WHAT KIND OF PARENT DO YOU ASPIRE TO BE, AND WHAT TRAITS DO YOU ADMIRE IN OTHER PARENTS THAT YOU'D LIKE TO DEVELOP IN YOURSELF?

HOW DID YOUR PARENTS HANDLE MONEY AND FINANCES IN RELATION TO YOUR UPBRINGING, AND WHAT VALUES AROUND MONEY DO YOU WANT TO INSTIL IN YOUR CHILD?

LOOKING BACK, WHAT'S ONE THING YOU WISH YOUR PARENTS HAD UNDERSTOOD BETTER ABOUT YOU, AND HOW CAN YOU BE MORE ATTUNED TO YOUR CHILD'S NEEDS?

WHAT VALUES WERE MOST IMPORTANT IN YOUR FAMILY GROWING UP, AND HOW DO YOU WANT TO PRIORITIZE THOSE VALUES IN YOUR PARENTING?

HOW DID YOUR PARENTS BALANCE WORK AND FAMILY LIFE, AND WHAT DO YOU ENVISION AS THE RIGHT BALANCE FOR YOU?

WHAT ROLE DID RELIGION OR SPIRITUALITY PLAY IN YOUR UPBRINGING, AND HOW DO YOU SEE IT SHAPING YOUR CHILD'S EXPERIENCE?

WHAT WAS THE BEST ADVICE YOUR PARENTS EVER GAVE YOU, AND HOW CAN YOU PASS THAT WISDOM ON?

WHAT BOUNDARIES DID YOUR PARENTS SET FOR YOU AS A CHILD, AND HOW DO YOU FEEL ABOUT SETTING BOUNDARIES FOR YOUR CHILD?

WERE THERE ANY SIGNIFICANT RULES IN YOUR HOUSEHOLD THAT YOU'D LIKE TO KEEP, CHANGE, OR NOT HAVE FOR YOUR CHILD?

HOW DID YOUR PARENTS APPROACH EDUCATION AND LEARNING, AND WHAT WILL YOUR APPROACH BE?

WHAT ARE SOME WAYS YOU CAN ENSURE YOUR CHILD FEELS CONFIDENT AND RESILIENT AS THEY GROW UP?

HOW DID YOUR FAMILY CELEBRATE MILESTONES, AND HOW DO YOU WANT TO CELEBRATE ACHIEVEMENTS AND SPECIAL MOMENTS WITH YOUR CHILD?

HOW DID YOUR PARENTS HANDLE MISTAKES OR FAILURES, AND HOW SHOULD YOU APPROACH THIS WITH YOUR CHILD?

WERE THERE ANY HABITS OR ROUTINES IN YOUR FAMILY THAT BROUGHT YOU CLOSER TOGETHER, AND HOW CAN YOU CREATE SIMILAR BONDS?

WHAT ROLE DO YOU SEE TECHNOLOGY PLAYING IN YOUR CHILD'S LIFE, AND HOW CAN YOU SET HEALTHY BOUNDARIES AROUND IT?

HOW CAN YOU TEACH YOUR CHILD TO VALUE KINDNESS AND EMPATHY?

WHAT KIND OF ROLE MODELS DO YOU WANT YOUR CHILD TO HAVE, AND HOW CAN YOU INTRODUCE THEM TO THOSE INFLUENCES?

HOW DID YOUR PARENTS HANDLE CELEBRATIONS LIKE BIRTHDAYS OR HOLIDAYS, AND HOW DO YOU ENVISION THOSE TRADITIONS IN YOUR FAMILY?

HOW CAN YOU FOSTER A SENSE OF INDEPENDENCE IN YOUR CHILD WHILE STILL OFFERING GUIDANCE AND SUPPORT?

HOW DID YOUR PARENTS APPROACH TOUGH CONVERSATIONS, AND WHAT'S YOUR PLAN FOR TACKLING THOSE WITH YOUR CHILD?

WHAT'S ONE THING YOU'RE EXCITED TO TEACH YOUR CHILD THAT REFLECTS YOUR OWN PASSIONS OR INTERESTS?

HOW DO YOU ENVISION BALANCING YOUR INDIVIDUAL PARENTING STYLES WITH THEIR OTHER CAREGIVERS TO CREATE A COHESIVE AND LOVING ENVIRONMENT FOR YOUR CHILD?

WHAT LESSONS ABOUT FRIENDSHIP DID YOU LEARN FROM YOUR PARENTS, AND HOW DO YOU WANT TO GUIDE YOUR CHILD IN FORMING HEALTHY RELATIONSHIPS?

HOW DID YOUR PARENTS HANDLE EMOTIONS OR STRESS, AND HOW CAN YOU CREATE A SUPPORTIVE EMOTIONAL ENVIRONMENT FOR YOUR CHILD?

WHAT WAS YOUR FAVORITE WAY TO SPEND THE WEEKENDS AS A FAMILY GROWING UP, AND HOW CAN YOU RECREATE SIMILAR MOMENTS?

HOW CAN YOU ENCOURAGE YOUR CHILD TO EMBRACE CURIOSITY AND A LOVE OF LEARNING?

WHAT ROLE DID CHORES OR RESPONSIBILITIES PLAY IN YOUR CHILDHOOD, AND HOW DO YOU SEE THEM FITTING INTO YOUR CHILD'S LIFE?

HOW DID YOUR FAMILY HANDLE BIG CHANGES OR TRANSITIONS, AND HOW CAN YOU HELP YOUR CHILD NAVIGATE THESE MOMENTS?

WHAT ARE SOME WAYS WE CAN TEACH YOUR CHILD GRATITUDE AND APPRECIATION FOR WHAT THEY HAVE?

HOW DO YOU THINK YOU CAN BALANCE ENCOURAGING YOUR CHILD TO TRY NEW THINGS WITHOUT PRESSURING THEM TOO MUCH?

WHAT'S ONE LESSON YOU'VE LEARNED AS AN ADULT THAT YOU WISH YOU'D KNOWN AS A CHILD, AND HOW CAN YOU PASS THAT ON?

HOW CAN YOU TEACH YOUR CHILD THE IMPORTANCE OF CARING FOR THE ENVIRONMENT AND CONTRIBUTING TO THEIR COMMUNITY?

WHAT FEARS DO YOU HAVE ABOUT NOT ALWAYS KNOWING THE 'RIGHT' PARENTING APPROACH, AND HOW MIGHT YOU LEARN TO TRUST YOUR INSTINCTS AS YOU GROW INTO THIS NEW ROLE?

ARE THERE MOMENTS WHEN YOU WORRY THAT YOUR OWN INSECURITIES OR UNRESOLVED CHILDHOOD ISSUES MIGHT AFFECT HOW YOU PARENT, AND WHAT STEPS CAN YOU TAKE TO PREVENT THAT?

HOW DO YOU PLAN TO HANDLE THE PRESSURE TO MEET SOCIETAL EXPECTATIONS OF A 'PERFECT PARENT'?

IN WHAT WAYS MIGHT YOU STRUGGLE WITH SETTING BOUNDARIES FOR YOUR CHILD, AND HOW CAN YOU PREPARE TO CONFIDENTLY SAY 'NO' WHEN IT'S NECESSARY?

HOW WILL YOU HANDLE FEELINGS OF GUILT THAT MAY ARISE IF YOU CANNOT ALWAYS PROVIDE EVERYTHING YOUR CHILD WANTS?

WHAT WILL YOU DO IF YOU FIND YOURSELF REPEATING PARENTING PATTERNS YOU ALWAYS VOWED TO AVOID, AND HOW CAN YOU BREAK FREE FROM THOSE INGRAINED HABITS?

HOW DO YOU INTEND TO MANAGE YOUR WORRIES ABOUT EXTERNAL INFLUENCES—SUCH AS MEDIA, ADVERTISEMENTS, OR PEER PRESSURE—WITHOUT BECOMING OVERLY CONTROLLING?

IF YOU ENCOUNTER UNCERTAINTY ABOUT HOW TO DISCUSS DIFFICULT TOPICS (LIKE DEATH, DISAPPOINTMENT, OR FAILURE) WITH YOUR CHILD, WHAT RESOURCES OR PREPARATION MIGHT HELP YOU FEEL MORE CONFIDENT?

WHAT CONCERNS DO YOU HAVE ABOUT TEACHING YOUR CHILD TO MANAGE THEIR OWN EMOTIONS, AND HOW CAN YOU MODEL HEALTHY EMOTIONAL REGULATION FOR THEM?

HOW MIGHT YOU COPE WITH THE FEAR OF YOUR CHILD FEELING LEFT OUT OR STRUGGLING SOCIALLY, AND HOW CAN YOU SUPPORT THEM THROUGH FRIENDSHIP CHALLENGES?

IF YOU FIND THAT YOUR PARENTING STYLE CLASHES WITH THAT OF YOUR PARTNER OR OTHER CAREGIVERS, HOW WILL YOU NAVIGATE THOSE DIFFERENCES TO MAINTAIN CONSISTENCY FOR YOUR CHILD?

HOW DO YOU THINK YOU'LL RESPOND TO MOMENTS WHEN YOU FEEL DISCONNECTED OR FRUSTRATED WITH YOUR CHILD, AND WHAT STEPS CAN YOU TAKE TO RECONNECT AND RESTORE UNDERSTANDING?

IF YOU START DOUBTING YOUR ABILITY TO PROVIDE THE GUIDANCE YOUR CHILD NEEDS, WHAT INNER STRENGTHS OR PAST EXPERIENCES CAN YOU DRAW UPON TO REASSURE YOURSELF?

HOW CAN YOU PREPARE FOR THE POSSIBILITY THAT YOUR CHILD MAY NOT SHARE YOUR INTERESTS OR VALUES, AND HOW WILL YOU RESPECT THEIR INDIVIDUALITY WHILE STILL GUIDING THEM?

WHAT STRATEGIES MIGHT YOU USE TO REMAIN PATIENT AND COMPASSIONATE WHEN YOUR CHILD'S BEHAVIOUR IS CHALLENGING?

HOW WILL YOU HANDLE YOUR ANXIETY ABOUT YOUR CHILD'S FUTURE, ESPECIALLY IF YOU WORRY THEY MIGHT FACE HARDSHIPS YOU NEVER EXPERIENCED YOURSELF?

IN WHAT WAYS CAN YOU PRACTISE SELF-KINDNESS ON DIFFICULT PARENTING DAYS, AND HOW MIGHT ACKNOWLEDGING YOUR OWN STRUGGLES IMPROVE YOUR RELATIONSHIP WITH YOUR CHILD?

WHAT WILL YOU DO WHEN YOU FEEL UNCERTAIN ABOUT WHETHER YOU'VE MADE THE RIGHT PARENTING CHOICES?

Printed in Dunstable, United Kingdom

66239029R00037